Level Up

How to Man Up and Excel When Society and
Role Models Have Let You Down

Original Edition

SAGE WILCOX

Level Up: How to Man Up and Excel When Society and Role Models Have Let You Down

Find Your Way Publishing, Inc.
P.O.Box 667
Norway, ME 04268
www.findyourwaypublishing.com

First Edition, 2018

ISBN-13: 978-1-945290-24-4

ISBN-10: 1-945290-24-2

Printed in the United States of America.

DEDICATION/ACKNOWLEDGEMENTS

This is dedicated to all the people who are working hard to better their lives and situations, day by day, in every way. Those who don't settle for mediocre will soar. Perseverance and discipline pays off. YOU deserve to make your dreams come true and reach your full potential, and this book is for you. Enjoy!

Deep, humble appreciation to the Divine Source, whom I aspire to grow closer to every day, in faith.

Thanks to all who made this book possible. And to those who share their stories and life experiences with me. Also, to those who loved and supported me as I worked on getting it published. You know who you are, and I am grateful.

And, most importantly, to the readers, thank you for taking the time to read this book. I hope you enjoy it and find something inside that resonates and inspires you in some way. If you find any of it beneficial please consider leaving a review. Reviews help more than you know. Thank you! Let's pour our favorite drink, find a comfortable spot, and get started, shall we? Our dreams and goals are waiting to be fulfilled.

Other books by Sage Wilcox:

Nonfiction:
Love Letters from Exes: *Proof That Life Goes on After a Break Up and Love Is What You Make It*

Get It Up: *101 Ways to Raise Your Vibration, Reduce Stress, Depression, & Anxiety, Increase Joy, Peace, & Happiness and Attract Abundance Automatically!*

The 2-Hour Vacation: *Let Go and Relax, Reduce Stress & Anxiety, Gain Inner Peace, and Happiness*

The Importance of Doing It: *How to Utilize Discipline to Get Out of Bed, and Make Your Dreams Come True! A Guide to Taking Action to Create Successful Habits, Reduce Stress, Anxiety, & Depression & Gain Self-Discipline, Motivation, & Success!*

Less Is Best: *Declutter, Organize, & Simplify to Reach Minimalism; Get More Time, Money, & Energy*

You Had Me at Re: Hello: *The Ultimate Guide to Online Dating, Including Tips and Testimonies*

Neuroplasticity and the Default Mind: *How to Shape Your Plastic Brain by Forming New Connections to Automatically Get Positive Results, Success and Prosperity*

Adjust: *How to Conquer and Accept Change and Adversity Swiftly; Stop Putting off the Love, Money, Peace, Success, and Happiness You Deserve Now*

Born New: *How to See the Familiar with New Eyes, Embrace the Magic of the Present Moment, Experience Satisfaction and Joy like Never Before*

Romance: Until We Fall
Under the Covers
Solitary Heart
Awakened Heart

Contents

Introduction

"Let men see, let them know, a real man, who lives as he was meant to live." ~ Marcus Aurelius

UNFORTUNATELY, BEING A MAN of character is not something that is taught in school. And unless one has the rare opportunity of being raised by such a man, then the odds are slim that these traits will naturally be passed on. In 2012 an article in the Washington Times stated that fifteen million, or 1 in 3 children from the U.S., live without a father. In Washington alone, 84 percent of children lived without a father in the home. In contrast, in 1960 it was just 11 percent.

So, what are the qualities that make a man, and how does one obtain them? As I work and talk with more and more people and families through the years, I've discovered that we have a lot to learn, men and women alike. Although I may put together a book, in the future, geared towards women, this book can help all who choose to read it. My research on this subject is vast and I've dedicated years to trying to discover what is needed to make all close relationships thrive. The characteristics that make a man a man can help carry and lead anyone to the top.

In today's society, more and more parents have to work more than one job simply to make ends meet. Where does this leave the children? It leaves them in the hands of busy daycare providers more and more of the time. Teachers and daycare providers, unfortunately, do not have the necessary one on one time needed to devote to each of these growing children. They also don't have the opportunity to be an example in the outside world. Yes, kids can learn a lot in a classroom, but there's a lot more to life, and if the parents aren't around (because they are working two or three jobs) then children lose out on important life learning opportunities. What I've found, more and more, is that a lot of young men haven't truly been taught how to be a man; a man of good character.

The issue of gender is unnecessarily complicated in today's politically correct environment. It is the price we pay for past mistakes in treating one gender subservient to the other. Being male is no more advantageous than being female, although you would not know that if you were to study the practices of some cultures today. With the majority of parents, in certain cultures, preferring sons over daughters, one only need to observe these traditions to get a sense of the way the feminine gender is perceived.

We are all guilty of it in one way or the other, men and women both. A vast majority of women look pejoratively on women deep in their hearts, and then go on to teach their sons and daughters the same.

We look at the role of a man, not from the perspective of a man, or the perspective of a woman. We look at the characteristics of a man's man from the perspective of the man who is one half of the full equation.

We have spent far too much time looking at man from the perspective of his sexuality and not enough time looking at him as part of something greater. This book walks through the steps that look at each characteristic endowment that man inherently has and the characteristics that he can build on top of that so that he can find fulfilment in his life by pursuing his purpose more effectively.

We all have dual purpose. One physical, and the other something far greater. The initial purpose is to form the basis of a family, which will launch the next generation, and to do that men must develop some of the characteristics that are based on the elements contained in the chapters of this book.

This book is designed to stimulate your own thought and to come to terms with what it means to be a man in your own world. You have to look deep inside yourself and find the real meaning of YOU. Tear away all the gender roles that have been cast upon you, the bad examples you've experienced, the commercial advertisements that define you based on material gain, and vanity. Cast aside the superficial things that don't matter and look at the things that really make a difference. You won't' find the answers anywhere else, to find them you need to look inside your own soul.

This book will provide you with a road map and include descriptions of the landmarks along the way. What you will discover and how long it takes you to get there is entirely up to you. That's the beauty of it. You are, after all, a unique individual and only you can find your own truth.

Most discussions that attempt to address the nature of being a man end up grazing the very notion that it seeks to stay away from. That notion is that there is a fundamental difference in man and woman, that makes a man a shade more capable, and which also makes a man the protector, the breadwinner and the leader.

This book stays away from all that. To embrace true equality, we first define the premise that it would be absolutely redundant to have two genders be identical to each other. Of course, there are some common physical attributes. Both genders share almost the same head, almost the same arms and legs, and almost the same heart, but many things are, of course, different.

As such, having two genders allows the species to increase in diversity as the population expands in number and across time. Without diversity, the species is in danger of extinction, especially a species that is as complex as ours. That is the whole point of gender. When you force two to combine to create the third, you create tremendous diversity.

So, from nothing came one, and from one came two - two genders, male and female. Both behave differently, both react differently, and both are usually categorized and eventually misjudged differently. While we may not all be the same, we are all sewn from the same fabric. Because of this, we are here together and should learn to lay out our differences not for the purpose of dispute, but for the purpose of communion.

Each of us plays a different role in this journey that lasts an average of 78 years. In that time not all of us can be the bus driver. Some of us have to be the conductor, others need to be the mechanic and so on. We are given different skills by the law of averages and together we make things happen. Hard workers are no more a blessing to the society than easy goers, we are just different, and we are all learning as we go, trying to live our lives successfully.

As much as I would like to take the time to go through both the genders and their interaction, to do so would lose the point of focusing on the qualities that make a man.

The first area of a man that we will cover is an important element, and it is something that even though is in us, needs to be cultivated and enhanced. The one true thing, in this life, that we are all given is the freedom to choose. That freedom is not just about having fries with your meal, but it's about how we want to proceed from one day to the next and what areas of our life we want to cultivate and enhance so that it increases our understanding of everything. Each of us is a candidate for enlightenment, but the path is not a compulsory one. It is a choice that we need to make and not everyone knows that it's available to them. Some may not even realize that's what they are looking for, some may call it by a different name, it may just be a feeling that something is missing or that there must be more to life. Regardless, it is a journey and one leg of the journey is about self-discovery. That's why you are reading this. There are no coincidences and you happen to be within the pages of this book because you are ready to dive deeper. You know deep down that you can have much more, and that you can be all that you were meant to be. To that end, we will first serve up the concept and nature of loyalty.

Take note, though, that the subject of loyalty, and indeed all the other subjects in the chapters that follow, while sounding like adjectives you have used a thousand times, however, they are not, and will differ from that which you are used to. As the chapters proceed you will see the reasoning behind this.

Once we have an understanding of loyalty, we need to look at honesty. Honesty is not just about telling the truth. It is about being the truth. When you are honest, it is because you have had the strength to make tough decisions along the way which allows you to speak honestly, seek honesty, and not escape or twist the truth. Honesty comes from strength. Strong people speak the truth because they are not afraid of it.

Honesty is about clarity of sight and the ability to see and convey things as they truly are. It can be a tricky proposition to be completely honest, and it is especially important that being a man is composed of events in your life that were the fruits of honesty. Without the honesty that pervades all things, it can become a murky mess and make it difficult to have any credibility and without credibility, it can become monumentally difficult to communicate the truth that others will believe. The lack of honesty will eventually erode your ability to remain functional or beneficial in your place in society.

Each person approaches the state of honesty from an individual and unique position. We do the same, but when we are deliberate in our approach then we can deliberately create and manifest our desired outcome. Look at honesty from a natural perspective and step away from the superficial. Chapter 2 will help you get a better understanding of it and that, in turn, will aid in creating your path.

The ending of Chapter 2 will set you up nicely to get an insight into why embracing the role of responsibility is so important and necessary. The true act of being responsible.

The word itself can convey a number of different kinds of responsibility. You will begin to see what the different roles are and how you can settle yourself into understanding them and taking them on. Chapter 3 delves deeper and goes beyond the everyday use of the word: responsibility; showing you how to maximize the benefits that come from it.

Once you tie together the state of being loyal to the art of being honest and the strength of being responsible you can then parlay all of those qualities into a person who will begin to contemplate a higher level of character and trustworthiness. That is the subject matter of Chapter 4. Chapter 4 also goes on to look at self-esteem (and how it is formed) which is an internal quality exhibited by external acts of honor - all the earmarkings of a man who is respectful and respected.

Chapter 5 looks at respect in a different light and charts out the reasons to be respectful and what exactly that entails. It also makes the case of using respect as something each man should aspire to get. This respect is received not by force but by contribution to the rest of mankind through actions.

The final three elements of being a man come rightfully at the end of the book. We set a separate chapter for being brave, and one for humility, and the last short chapter is on strength.

Every chapter that is presented here offers you a different perspective than you would traditionally find. The elements here are designed to introduce and stimulate simultaneously, they are designed to bring fact to your own brand of execution and together you will be able to understand that what makes a man is already within you.

Unfortunately, this is not something that is taught in school, however, and thankfully, all we need is a little guidance in the right direction. That direction is not up or down, left or right, but instead, you will realize that we are trying to point you inwards - into the depths of your own soul which is where you will find your own truth. And from there you will easily be able to implement the tools within this book to reach your full destiny.

***

Chapter 1: Loyalty

"Within the hearts men, loyalty and consideration are esteemed greater than success." ~ *Bryant H. McGill*

A MAN WEARS DIFFERENT HATS throughout his life, just as a woman does. We all go through stages of physical growth, levels of psychological maturity and shades of spirituality. Just as these personal characteristics have attributes, our interactional social life has its own characteristics as well. An individual is just one piece in the entire puzzle, and he is not isolated from the other pieces of the puzzle. Instead, he forms a functional bond between himself and the universe he comes into contact with around him.

This functional bond has various levels of strength, and depends on how the relationship manifests and how long it has been in development. This bond is what we refer to as loyalty. For a man, this loyalty is an important aspect of who he is and what he will grow into.

There are three dimensions to a man's loyalty. The first is his loyalty evidenced by his actions; then there is the loyalty projected by his words, and finally, the loyalty conjured in his thoughts. It may be a little confusing to see loyalty expressed in terms that are attributed to thought, word, and deed, but, in essence, true loyalty is composed of elements that manifest in these three states of existence.

Loyalty to and of Thought

The first step begins as a thought. Whether that thought mirrored learned experience or was instilled instruction, doesn't matter. The first seed, from a self-centric perspective, is from within the framework of the mind. Loyalty must be the mindset that encapsulates all other thoughts when it comes to family, friend's, work ethic, you name it.

When it comes to the mind, there is loyalty to thought and loyalty of thought. The two describe the bond between the self and the action but are applied to different actions.

Loyalty of thought is the notion that there is no entertaining of thoughts to be disloyal, or that break the bond, between oneself and a friend, family member, or loved one.

Loyalty to thought is the ability to think of something and have the courage, will, and strength to pursue the thought to actioned completion. Loyalty in this sense is different from will to complete or the mental fortitude to act. It simply means that a person holds the ideas and cherishes the idea behind the act so deeply that they will not abandon it in the face of opposition, temptation or difficulty. Loyalty to thought or idea, or ideals, are just differing scopes of the same notion.

The second kind of loyalty - loyalty of thought is where your thoughts are loyal to something external to yourself. For instance, a man can be loyal to his spouse by not cheating on her with another person. However, if he fantasizes about another person constantly, he is not being loyal to thought and is cheating on his wife in his mind. One is the act, the other is the thought. Loyalty of thought means that the man's thoughts do not betray the bond that exists between him and the person he is loyal to.

Loyalty of Word

Words are the juxtaposition in most cases between thought and deed. It is not necessarily something that is spoken or written, it can be something assumed, or something that is intimated, something that is set by precedent or something that is contrived from convention. Whatever form it manifests in, as long as it is the shadow of loyalty that comes just prior to the act of loyalty and just after the thought of loyalty, then it satisfies the necessary conditions to be considered as loyalty of word.

A man's word is indeed his bond, covenant, promise. When he utters the words or in any way transmits the message that he is saying something, then the action that follows from there must be true as well. The loyalty of word is entwined within the concept and the meaning of the man.

The issue of loyalty is a highly important thread in the fabric of every man. Not only is it a display of will, but it is also the evidence of a refined man of character, and the hallmark of a strong mind. The loyalty of word is especially a true test because men with less than what it takes to be a man are usually very cavalier with their words. And it's not just the choice of words that bear testimony to a man, but also his gesture, tone, and the gravity in its delivery.

A man of good fiber has evidence of loyalty to thought and is perceptibly loyal to deed. How he crafts his words, and the manner in which his loyalty to words is evident, is a good prognosticator of the actions that will follow.

We are instinctively drawn to men of strong words, we are enthralled by men who write and deliver iconic speeches. We assume eloquence to mean greatness. This assumption of ours comes from the fact that we value loyalty to words and when we see that trait in another man we attach that same value to his mind, and to his potential deeds.

Loyalty to word is not just about what you say, but it is also about what you don't say. A strong man who is measured, treats discourse, private or public, casual or formal, with a sense of purpose and is careful not to betray the trust placed in him by knowing when to say the right thing, but by also knowing when not to say the wrong thing. Loyalty to word is a man who chooses his words carefully.

Loyalty of Action

Before we come upon action, even action born in impulse, and especially action marinated in thoughtful consideration, we observe that it stems from the processes of the mind. Like the act of being loyal to one's environment and community and the structures that uphold it and protect it. Loyalty in action, the final form of loyalty that makes a difference and has an impact to those that share the environment is evidence of what goes on in the person's mind and by extension the measure by which future actions can be determined.

Loyalty is a matter of balance, especially when viewed from the perspective of action. On one end of the spectrum, that describes the effects and nature of loyalty, you find loyalty born out of altruism; on the other end of the spectrum, you find loyalty born out of self-importance - or selfishness.

We often think of the two ends of the spectrum as something that describes polar opposites. Indeed, even the way the interaction between the two are represented here seems to suggest that they are diametrically opposed. But what they really are is just a matter of degrees.

The length of the shadow man casts on his environment is a function of the time horizon of the action the man has contemplated. Usually acts that are more selfish in nature cast short shadows - meaning they are designed to harvest the efforts of man within a short time horizon and have the least number of beneficiaries. Actions with a seemingly more altruistic intention are actions that impact a larger number of beneficiaries or people in his environment around him. In other words, selfish acts benefit fewer people, whereas meaningful acts do and will benefit more people. It is fairly simple and makes perfect sense when you think about it. A man of good character will think before he acts.

Of course, self-interest is an essential part of the survivability of the human species. It has to be. If not, the human species would eventually cease to exist. What is in contention then is not the act that flows from self-interest but rather the act that flows from balance that takes into account the loyalty man has to different objects in his environment.

The greater the difference in a person's loyalty to objects in his environment the easier the decision to make. The closer they are the harder the decision. For instance, a man's loyalty to his children is greater than his loyalty to other objects in his environment, say a stray cat. If the man is driving fast around a corner and as he emerges from the blind turn he spots his daughter just to the left of center and a stray cat just to the right of center. He will not hesitate to swerve right, into the cat. His loyalty to his family member is significantly more than his loyalty to life in general or the stray cat's life. The decision is easy.

If, however, you replace the cat in this illustration with something that has the same loyalty factor, let's say you replace the unfortunate feline with another of his daughters, then his easy decision to swerve right vanishes and he is thrust into a situation that presents no solution.

Man bases most of his decisions on the level of importance he places on all of the objects in his environment. This priority balance sheet determines what ranks higher in his decision making process and, as such, has an influence on his decisions.

Man's decisions and actions are impacted when he has a poor understanding of the attributes of the object in his environment or if he has poor ability in assigning loyalty to that object. For instance, many policy makers in our government's halls of power have no appreciation for the degradation of nature's environment. In this case, that lack of appreciation leads them to not treat its potential effects with any credible sense of urgency. Some suggest that it is a problem with the lack of understanding the science. Others contend that their loyalties lie elsewhere.

Visualizing Loyalty

The start of loyalty begins deep within the male psyche. He is first and foremost built to be loyal to no external subject. His only loyalty, in the beginning, is to his internal self. But that changes over time as he ages, he starts to grow, learn, understand, and visualize that loyalty.

When you are a man, you learn to take the high road and make choices that will allow you to keep all your priorities while remaining loyal to both; things that are of a selfish and an altruistic nature. You have to visualize loyalty as a decision driven event rather than an option driven uncertainty.

Loyalty is the product of strength, intellect, and the desire to take responsibility ahead of an event. It requires honesty, which we will discuss in the next chapter; and it requires respect for all things. It requires wisdom that is gained from reflection along with resolve.

Manifesting Loyalty

When all is said and done what we see is that each person's profile is made up of degrees of loyalties across a spectrum of choices. As we grow in mind, body, and spirit, that balance evolves. The ideal picture of a man's loyalty profile is one that is able to occupy a larger spread of the spectrum and effectively take care of things at home and abroad, internally and externally, big and small.

One must manifest loyalty by understanding our role in society and then expanding our portfolio of things that we are loyal to, instead of replacing one with another. We must be able to be selfish and selfless at the same time. We must be able to take care of our ward and the environment simultaneously.

***

Chapter 2: Honesty

"Honesty is the first chapter in the book of wisdom"
~ Thomas Jefferson

LET'S START WITH AN illustration of the term honesty. Let's imagine two individuals. One makes a promise and the other is the person the promise is made to, and he is totally dependent on that promise and expects with one hundred percent certainty that the promise will come to fruition.

At the prescribed time, the promise is broken because the person who made the promise is unable to fulfill his end of the bargain. Regardless of whether the circumstances that precipitated the breaking of the promise was foreseeable, avoidable, or minor, the fact remains that the promise was broken.

Who, in this illustration would you consider to be the dishonest one?

Obviously, the one who made the promise, right? Well, most people, and even I until a short time ago, would tell you without any hesitancy that it is the person who broke the promise who is dishonest. No one with any shred of decency would say otherwise. However, in truth, both can be labeled as dishonest.

The person in this illustration who made the promise is not dishonest just because he didn't fulfill his promise, but also because he did not foresee the events accurately enough to make the promise in the first place. As for the second person, the receiver of the promise, he is equally to blame because he gave an expectation to an event that had not yet occurred.

If you find the definition of honesty here to be confusing, that is understandable. Honesty is best understood at a level that penetrates the superficial. To really understand what it means, to be honest, you have to look at the nature of being honest and the framework from where the opportunity, to be honest, comes from, or otherwise presents itself. Yes, honesty means being truthful, but there is more to it than that.

A man, someone who is true to his place in the world and to the purpose of his species, gender, and society understands instinctively that honesty is much more than just telling the truth. It is more than fulfilling a promise and it is more than paying a debt on time.

Nature of Honesty

The nature of honesty is instinctively known to each of us. Regardless of gender, regardless of age, human beings are generally honest. This honesty is predicated on equity. There is a sense of fairness in nature that you see occur in the circle of life. A lion will not hunt a prey if it is not hungry or threatened. That is the nature of nature and lions are generally honest creatures, so are snakes, eagles, and other predators.

The human nature of honesty, however, has evolved, and it is currently in a state of flux to the point that people are expected to be true to their promise even when it goes against their true nature. This is not necessarily a good thing or a bad thing, and once we learn to accept this then we can begin to understand the true nature of honesty. Without this, any hope or intention that we may have about being honest will be in vain and ultimately dishonest in itself.

Dishonesty doesn't feel right, and is unhealthy for our bodies as well. This is why lie detectors can, at times, indicate and predict when someone is lying. Our blood pressure, respiration, heart rate, amongst other things, changes when we are lying. Something fires off in our bodies when we are dishonest, physical responses that normally wouldn't be happening internally if we were being honest and these reactions can literally be measured and recorded.

Unfortunately, the more one lies, the easier it can become to lie again and again. Some people have formed a habit of being dishonest. They tell one little white lie after another. Once your family and friends feel as though they can't trust you it can become extremely difficult to regain their trust back again. They will question almost everything you say and do because you've been dishonest in the past. A real man learns to choose his words carefully and says what he means. A real man is strong enough to tell the truth in all situations, big and small. He is not afraid to be honest, and he has gained the trust of those around him.

Nature of Life

The human conscious mind is still grappling with what it means to be human and what our purpose here is. We have deciphered many mysteries, but we must realize humbly that we have a long way to go.

The nature of life in itself is simple. It is based on a journey of discovery and on realizing that we are all connected. The connection is not just between humans, or only between a subset of a species or only between living things. No, instead we are all connected to everything. Hydrogen, oxygen, carbon and a bunch of other elements manifest today as your physical body. These same elements, at some point in the future, will manifest as rain, roots of a tree, part of the soil, and whatever else lies in its future. That is the nature of life - we are all connected, and we are all continually learning.

Once we understand that we are all connected, then all we have to do is realize that we are all equal. This perspective of equity is the energy that powers the nature of life. We are all equal but sometimes ego and its notion that one is better than the other can be the cause for many problems.

The ego steps in, and in an effort to inflate itself, steps away from a lot of the characteristics that make a real man. The first on the hit list is the ability to be honest with one's own self and the ability to be truthful to those around. All in the pursuit of something that may not even be real.

The ego is also the main culprit for not taking responsibility for one's actions; actions that have been determined to be mistakes in one's life. The irony is that life's mistakes are the best way of learning and when one does not admit to a mistake, one cannot and does not learn from it. The ego, in the end, blocks the person from actually learning and growing. There is a limited need to the ego because it allows one to identify the jurisdiction of his command and control. It creates a sense of ownership over one's self. But beyond that, the ego becomes an impediment that pushes the self-importance and self-worth beyond its rightful borders of the self.

When these parts of the mind, the one that delineates the extent of the ego, the intellectual side that understands that we are all connected, and the subconscious side which knows the truth, all come together, then we are able to be truly honest about all things without the superficial nonsense that many labor under.

To be a man of character, one needs this kind of honesty. This is the honesty that does not rely on a simple promise but understands the extent of each person's words. Imagine lending your brand new car to someone who doesn't know how to drive, based simply on the promise that they will bring it back undamaged. If you lend your car to them against your better judgment, who is really to blame if the car comes back damaged? You share equally in the blame because you were not honest with yourself when you went against your better judgment and believed the person who borrowed your vehicle.

Honesty is not about being cynical. It's simply about being honest. When you seek this kind of honesty, you will slowly develop the ability to see things the way they are. The more you avoid the truth and deny things for what they are, or the more you justify your actions to suit your misguided wants, needs, or false beliefs, then, unfortunately, you can easily be duped into anything. The truth becomes harder to see when you continually avoid it. But when you seek honesty for what it is then you will slowly develop the ability to see the truth more and more and in every situation.

Honesty goes both ways. If you are strong you can be honest. Strength is a major part of being honest especially being honest with yourself, and with others.

***

Chapter 3: Responsibility

"You cannot evade the responsibility of tomorrow by evading it today." ~ Abraham Lincoln

WE HAVE LOOKED AT THE FIRST two foundations of manning up. The depth of loyalty and the span of honesty are not enforced by anyone or anything except the whip of consequence. The key is to learn to foresee the possible calamity that awaits the person who has yet to instill the characteristics that make up the soul of a real man.

It is our responsibility as grown adults to do what we need to do so that we can gain the necessary elements that will allow us to be functional and purposeful in life.

Responsibility is what governs us internally, and directs our actions externally. If one hasn't learned, therefore, lacks the necessary skills and responsibility required to take on the characteristics described in earlier chapters (and characteristics that will be described in later chapters) then what inevitably happens is that one will not be able to see things as they are and, therefore, not be able to make rational and necessary decisions. This will eventually impact one's life and the consequences that befall may not be entirely agreeable.

There are basically three levels of responsibility. The first is a menial level of responsibility; this is where you do things for yourself without being forced to. It's like getting a first grader to do their homework without being told or reminded. This type of responsibility is learning what needs to happen and taking action to get it done without being forced or told to.

The second type of responsibility is the responsibility to shoulder and care for others who depend on you. As a responsible adult, you will find that there is a time when you need to take responsibility for the safety and well being of those around you, from the inanimate objects in your home, to your children and family, and right down to your pet cat.

Taking on this sort of responsibility means that you put yourself in a position where you stand in front of the inevitable. You learn to put others before yourself and stand up and face the task at hand with maturity, knowing that certain decisions require one to take necessary action and follow through.

The final kind of responsibility is very important. It is about taking responsibility in all things. It's about taking responsibility when things go wrong or when we make unfavorable choices. This kind of responsibility is about looking at mistakes that happen in your sphere of influence and then, no matter how remote, taking responsibility for your part in it, even if you aren't entirely to blame. Just like the example I shared earlier of an inexperienced driver asking to use your brand new car. If you agreed to let that person use your vehicle and they crash it, then you are partly responsible because you said yes. The mature person takes responsibility for all areas of their lives and does not place blame on others for anything.

Why is it important to practice taking full responsibility in all areas of our lives? The reason is because doing so will condition you to expand your sphere of influence. When you take on the area around you, you are taking control of what happens. This control is not the conscious grab for power, but the noble act of taking responsibility for every part of your life.

There is a big difference in the three ways responsibility manifests itself in a person's life. A "real man" can clearly take on all three.

The higher level of responsibility allows you to learn the most important lessons in which you will reap many benefits. This fact is predicated on the way the mind works. If you place the mind in a position where it has to work its way out of something it will do one of two things. It will either take full responsibility and solve the issue, or it will place the blame elsewhere and take a dishonest route around it. Strong people take full responsibility for every issue in their lives. This is the function of strength. If you are strong enough, then you will go through it, if you are too weak then you will go around it.

By taking responsibility for something and learning from it today, you avoid it from happening again tomorrow. Shining the light of truth on your life will help clear the path for your future. This strategy of learning requires strength and honesty.

Obviously, when we say to take full responsibility for every little detail of your life, we are not talking about confessing to murder if you are in no way the cause of it. What we are talking about has to do within your personal setting where you stand up as the man to see and accept what your role is, in things that go wrong, at the personal and work level.

For example, when you learn to take responsibility for your part in a simple argument, a number of things happen. For one, you relieve the pressure that builds up between all participants in the argument, allowing things to be resolved quickly and in a peaceful manner. When it comes to mistakes made within your family, you will undoubtedly start to identify better ways to take full responsibility for your part and learn from it. Your subconscious makes a note of it and when sequences of events are similar, it will alert you to a possible outcome so that you can take responsibility and then do something to alter the chain of events in a more positive way.

At the same time, do not take responsibility for things that may rob someone else of learning. It is important that we all learn to take full responsibility for our own part in all things, but unfortunately, not all will learn this, therefore, we must focus on our part. We can't control what other people do, but we can learn to not let others get to us. It's important to let others off the hook when it comes to how we feel. Real men do not let the actions or insensitivities of others steal their joy in any way. When we allow others to upset us, we must learn to take full responsibility in the fact that we allowed it, and then practice releasing that control (we offered up freely to them) by pausing and reminding ourselves that we get to choose how we feel regardless of what is going on around us. Real men have mastered this. No one can make them upset, frustrated, or angry without their consent.

As a man, there is no shame in taking responsibility for a mistake. When you take responsibility, you get the benefit of being the better person and you get the benefit of never making the same mistake again. Once we acknowledge and take full responsibility for a mistake, we bring it to light allowing us to move forward and progress. It's when we hide our mistakes that they tend to take hold of us and we fall into the trap of repeating the same mistakes over and over.

Mistakes are designed to teach us. All it requires is that we admit that we made a mistake and learn from it. That's why taking responsibility for mistakes, and taking responsibility for all things within our sphere of influence and being responsible in thought, word, and deed is important in being a man. A "real man" easily admits to his mistakes, learns and grows from them, and does not make the same mistake twice.

***

Chapter 4: Trustworthy

"Depend upon yourself. Make your judgment trustworthy by trusting it. You can develop good judgment as you do the muscles of your body - by judicious, daily exercise. To be known as a man of sound judgment will be much in your favor." ~ *Grantland Rice*

TO BE A MAN MEANS that you owe it to yourself and to the world at large to be trustworthy. There are two factors involved in becoming and being trustworthy. The first factor is that you need to have the correct amount of self-esteem so that you realize that you are indeed worth every measure that you aspire to be. The second is that who you are inside matters a lot, but how you translate what's inside into action matters more.

Self Esteem

It's hard to get a grip on what self-esteem means, and what it entails simply because this term, at times, has been trivialized to mean something less significant and less useful than it really is.

Self-esteem in its own right is a term that is rather subjective. It remains in the mind of the person invoking the term and when communicated in the absence of detailed explanation, it can convey the wrong profile.

To be clear self-esteem is the value you hold yourself in. That value is not a subjective notion but rather one that is determined by your subconscious. Your conscious brain, when asked to weigh in, would most naturally inflate what yourself worth may be. However, we are not interested so much in what your conscious mind has to opine (or suggest or say) about the matter.

What we are really interested in is the opinion of your subconscious because that is what really matters in the projection of your self-esteem. But to know what your subconscious feels in terms of its definition of yourself is not a direct process. You can get a better understanding of your subconscious in one of two ways. First, you can observe your actions and see what and where they point to. The second is by spending a significant amount of time reflecting on the nature of your thoughts, the effects and consequences of your past actions and the mistakes that you have made in the past, or continue to make.

When looking at your level of self-esteem you can make a determination of how effective and sufficient yours is by looking at the nature of your past. If you are the kind of person who has always been full of self-confidence and therefore, successful, then you probably have more than your average share of self-esteem. A person with unshakeable self-esteem is one who is not afraid to dive in, and bring all the elements together to manifest in the result that is envisioned.

Action

The second step is action. To be a person who is trustworthy you must be able to match your plan with action and bring it to fruition. Being trustworthy means that when you say something you do it. Ideally, you do what you say when you say it.

Action is the defining moment of this entire equation. It is only by action that we get to see the innermost thought process of the character inside. It is also via inaction that we get to read the person. Being trustworthy is very important because it builds credibility for the future and that credibility leads to other opportunities. I must add that it is also important because it feels good. When one can trust themselves to take the appropriate action they have reached a freedom like no other. This type of trustworthiness is priceless and real men attain it.

These are the two main ingredients that go into the making of trustworthiness; self-esteem and action. Along with these, there are other ingredients that take lesser time but should also be included to be able to give your brand of trustworthiness the correct consistency it needs to take hold.

Trustworthiness is about one's ability to promise only what he is able to deliver.

***

Chapter 5: Respect

"Openness, respect, integrity - these are principles that need to underpin pretty much every other decision that you make." ~ Justin Trudeau

LET'S DISPENSE WITH AND get rid of the presumption that showing respect is a sign of weakness, or that it is some form of kowtowing. It can be interpreted as such if you deliver the token of respect with such passive and deprecating tones. But it doesn't have to be, and it must not be. How you deliver your respect says a lot about who you are, and how you got to where you are.

Another aspect that you should consider in your endeavor to be respectful, and maintain respect, is that you will need to show respect consistently and display the same amount of respect in all situations. That's the whole point and real men have mastered it. You should not be method acting your signs of respect. Instead, and with practice, you will start to truly feel respectful towards others, and in all situations, and then all you need to do is allow those sincere feelings to show.

Being respectful starts as a choice, where your tone, gesticulations, adherence to moral and ethical principles, and your choice of topic and vocabulary can move from uncomfortable distractions to practiced indifference. Indifferent in the sense that no matter what is going on around you, you will remain respectful at all times. Real men set aside their opinions and formed beliefs and are respectful regardless. From this point forward, as you practice with increased frequency you will be released into the general population to test your skills at being respectful to others, and it will become easier and easier and more natural. Practice makes perfect.

Reasons for Being Respectful

Being respectful, in different cultures, is practiced for different reasons and in different ways. But there is one of two categories that each mark of respect could easily be dropped into. One is external, which is where you show respect to a person in forms of rituals; for instance, men tipping their hats as they pass a lady in old westerns. Those acts are rituals of respect. The second is when you experience, internally, a grateful appreciation for a person's wisdom and guidance in your life.

Both these categories encapsulate every form of respect that human nature and human culture have evolved over time. There is something deep within our mental framework that yearns to pay respect to those whom we revere and to those who protect us, guide us, and care for us. It is not the bond of love, it is not the fraternity of friendship, and it is not the kinship of kindness. It is a naturally occurring phenomena that has been formalized in many cultures and it is even encoded in many present-day religions. In the Bible, for instance, the mark of respect is characterized by the commandment of children honoring their parents.

It turns out that being respectful creates a situation where the party who is showing the respect is able to learn better from the party that is being respected. Human beings have this state of being respectful in specific relationships. In some relationships, it is mutually exclusive and in other relationships it is mutual. But for the most part being respectful is a matter of degrees.

For instance, a young child has a high level of respect for his or her teachers. The teachers have a mutual respect for their students but to a different degree. But that degree of respect expands and increases over time while the child's respect evolves as he matures.

Most people misunderstand the benefit of being respectful. Respect is the natural currency between two human beings regardless of their relative stations in life. A parent's guidance and wisdom are bartered in exchange for the child's respect. The worker's respect towards his superior is because of the flow of information and direction to the employee from the boss. When you look at it from this perspective you start to get a hint of the nature of respect. It starts to become clear that when you pay respect you have an advantage in terms of what the other gives in return.

That kind of respect can be voluntary, or it can be extracted forcefully. There is also a kind of respect that grows once a person displays his proficiency in a certain field. This form of respect is the natural way we can open a window of understanding into another person's field of mastery.

Being an effective man requires that you gain both sides of respect. You have to know when to give it and when to demand it. But the trick here is that you do not demand it by force, you demand it by giving something in return for it.

As a man when you do all that you have to do to protect, raise and provide for your family, maternal or matrimonial, you automatically gain the respect of your wards and family members. This shows that you are on the right track. When you do the right thing, you may not be popular at times, but you will always be respected. This respect does not need to always be fully displayed or exhibited but you know that it is there. Respect does not in any way imply affection or love.

When I was growing up we had a Discipline Master that made sure the students were properly behaved. Any misbehavior, anything from tardiness to untidy hair to other transgressions typical of high school students, would earn a visit to the Principal's office. Mr. Miller was the most feared and disliked member of the faculty of any person there. But the one thing that he had was the unmistakable respect in thought, word, and deed of every student in school. His methods, as unorthodox as they may have been, imparted many of the qualities that all of us, since then, have needed to do well in life. We feared him all those years, but we respected him, naturally. We were not prodded into showing respect, we did it voluntarily. As we grew older, we began to appreciate him more because we realized how much his guidance benefited us. The respect we felt in every fiber of our body was the currency that mirrored the value we placed on his guidance.

A funny thing happens as your respect for a person grows, whatever they have to impart in ways of teaching and guidance begins to stick even more as time goes on. The same is true for relationships between teacher and student, parent and child. When we give respect we get the fuller measure of their respect and guidance in return.

Real men respect others deeply from whom they know they can learn a lot. When we are open to learning in all moments and from all people and experiences then respect will flow naturally. It is unfortunate that hatred can block respect and when it does we are left out in the cold. Hatred blocks our respect for others, and hinders us from seeing the wisdom of the other person's guidance and then we lose every benefit that may have flowed from it.

The reverse is also true. As men and women, we are tasked with the imparting of knowledge from our unique perspective to others around us. But when we act in certain ways that are unacceptable to those within our gravity, we lose the ability to have a positive impact on other lives. This is especially true for fathers who make a number of wrong moves and fall by the wayside. Immediately following their fall from grace, the respect that they once held is eroded and unfortunately, the natural consequence from that is that their words will no longer carry any weight.

Commanding respect is not done by wielding fear. It comes from having something to offer the other person. When a statesman tirelessly looks out for his citizens he is respected. When a parent guides his child through the maze of life, he is respected, when a man contributes to his fellow man, he is mutually respected.

Since respect is a currency that facilitates the interaction between us, the fact that we also realize that every single person, every single living thing, every single creation; from plants, to land, to creatures, big and small, all have something to offer us in terms of knowledge and guidance, and have something to offer us in the physical realm of things as well. For this reason, we need to pay respect to every single one of them. When we lose our prejudice, when we learn the truth, when we start to see every object in our environment with eyes that recognize each individual's value, we are compelled to pay respect to all things around us. When we do, we begin to learn more than we can possibly imagine.

As a man, we need to teach this respect to our children; we need to pay this respect to all, and we should receive this respect for the role we play. We get what we give, we reap what we sow.

***

Chapter 6: Bravery

*"A true knight is braver in the midst, than in the
beginning of danger."* ~ *Sir Philip Sidney*

WE UNDERESTIMATE BRAVERY each time we
overestimate the fear that arises before it. Being brave is
never a state that we are born into, it is a condition that we
learn to invoke. We need to look at this condition as we
would a tree. A tree that does not experience the fury of
gusting winds, bending this way and that, will grow slender
and tall. Never being challenged in its existence, a strong
wind coming later in its life could break it mid-trunk and
forever kill the tree. But in comparison, a tree that since
young is subjected to high winds that bend it and rustle it,
constantly, daily even, starts to grow stronger roots and a
stronger and more flexible trunk. The tree grows stronger
in the face of adversity.

Bravery is like that tree, it is unable to grow and fortify
itself in the absence of adversity. The adversity that builds
bravery the most is one that invokes various kinds of fear.
Fear is not an external emotion, it is an internal warning
system. Fear is the warning system that a person is getting

uncomfortably close to a situation that will impress and endanger his ability to fulfill his purpose. Fear is an indicator that we are expanding out of our comfort zone. What we do with this fear is up to us. We can embrace it and move forward and as we do we become braver and braver.

Until he faces occasion to invoke bravery, he is still a boy. A man encapsulates all the characteristics described in the preceding chapters and then has to use those to navigate his way out of situations that cause him to feel a sense of fear. From a natural perspective not only does man have a strong sense of fear, but man is also endowed with the necessary physical and hormonal balance to counter fear though logic, reasoning and physical strength.

Fear

Fear is an electrochemical response originating in the base of the brain in an area that is almost as old as the rudimentary central nervous system. Because the rest of the brain is built on top of it, the fear center of the brain is hardwired into every other part of the brain and in essence is a major influence in every aspect of our lives.

Everything that happens to us filters through the fear center and that is the reason fear is one of the greatest motivators we have. However, as time passed we started to label fear as the mark of the weak and consequently, we labeled those who do not display fear as being strong. This is disastrous to the natural order of things. Fear is a powerful ally when it's tempered with reason and logic because aside from alerting us with that familiar sensation of being scared or that feeling of being anxious, fear also activates a physical response in our body. It pumps up the necessary hormones and it gets the heart going so as to deliver a higher blood pressure, and thereby, increasing oxygen saturation to our muscles and brain.

Fear, in essence, is responsible for triggering the fight, flight, or freeze response. In the wake of stimuli that possibly endangers our being and our purpose, we get into one of these three modes. The body is prepared to fight in the event that we subconsciously analyze that the threat can be vanquished; we get into flight mode if we realize that our chances of survival in a fight are low and we flee instead. However, if we are faced with a situation, in ancient times that would mean facing a predator, then what happens is that we automatically freeze. Freezing, and looking as though we are dead, disinterests the predator who eventually walks away.

For better or for worse that is the set of physical attributes that have been handed down to us, except that today we face threats, existential or otherwise, in very different forms. However, the mind still treats unfavorable consequences with a fear response. And increasingly, the problems that we face end up not having instant and pre-prescribed solutions. This results in many people going into a state of 'freeze' or in other words anxiety attacks.

When it comes to men, there is no shortage of fear that can get bottled up because of the ego, which comes into play and needs to project a certain kind of stature. That in turn, when bottled up, results in it eating away at the soul and health of the man. You can evidence this by the shorter average life expectancy that men generally face.

For a man, especially as one who looks after his family, it is in his best interest and it is his responsibility to keep himself healthy so that he can provide the necessary protection and support for his family. Real men have learned, with practice, to do this.

Bravery is not the inability to feel fear, but rather the ability to understand the source of fear and harvest the energy that it gives to channel it in the direction that will solve the problem at hand. That's what being brave is. Being brave is sometimes also mischaracterized as the opposite of freezing or panicking. This is not entirely true, except in the sense where it means that you use the fear that arises to alert you that something is amiss, and you find the strength within and use your wits about you to get it fixed.

A man needs to be brave so that he can carry the responsibilities that face him at every turn. This ability to be brave is not the bravado that men sometimes exhibit. That bravado is mostly an overcompensating mask that manifests when the man is unable to figure a cogent way forward. But this is not a bad thing as long as it does not become habitual.

Momentary bravado is fine because the human condition works on inner and outer interplay. We are subject to the outward action of an inward grace where we are constantly getting one side of the equation started by controlling the other side. Sometimes when you long to be happy, you smile outwardly first, or you dance to music that makes you feel better. Sometimes people think that you dance because you feel great. In actual fact, you should also dance when you feel bad because the outward action of dancing will elevate your inward mood as well.

***

Chapter 7: Humility

"Humility is the solid foundation of all virtues." ~
Confucius

BEING HUMBLE IS THE THREAD that binds all the previous characteristics and is the closest kin of being respectful. From humility respect sprouts because you will not be able to display respect to others if you cannot muster up the ability to invoke humility.

What is humility? Humility is the act of being humble. A person is said to be humble when they do not think themselves to be higher than another person. Another way to look at it is to remember that humility is the antitheses or direct opposite of pride. Do not confuse pride with being proud.

Humility is a necessary condition to learn and to learn effectively. If you are not able to invoke humility you will not be able to overcome the wall that most people usually build around themselves in the process of aiding their ego in defining their personality.

When we refer to the vanquishing of the ego and the pride that is constituent with it, what we are really talking about is the balancing of humility with pride.

This is the most important characteristic of man. It is imperative that a man is able to institute balance and keep from swinging from one extreme to the next. Extreme behavior, whether defined as good or bad, can both be problematic. Too much 'good' can be more disastrous than a little 'bad'.

Humility is a key ingredient in being respectful, which is the key ingredient in learning, and together these guide you to be a better man.

***

Chapter 8: Strength

"The real man smiles in trouble, gathers strength from distress, and grows brave by reflection." ~ *Thomas Paine*

THE STRENGTH WE ARE referencing here is not the number of barbells that you can lift or the speed in which you can run a mile. The strength of a real man is plainly and simply the amount of time you continue to be brave in the face of continuous stimulus that raises fear; it is the number of times you pick yourself up after falling time and again; it is the number of times you try until you finally succeed. Strength is what keeps you going when you make mistakes. Strength is continually learning the ins and outs of this life, applying what we learn, and ultimately what makes a person successful.

All the elements of this book, from loyalty to humility, require repeated display and practice in the face of everyday adversities and challenges. This is where strength comes into play. If you can't hold up against the assaults, then all the characteristics we have discussed here become merely academic with no real world application or use.

You need to build your strength and you do that by the power of decisions. You make a decision to do something and you do it, you follow through, and don't let go under any reasonable circumstances.

In the physical world we live in, strength in the arm is measured by how much force we can apply. We gauge that by the weight of what we can push or by how much we can lift. One is utilized by the resistance and the other by the will.

To be able to build muscle strength you do two things. One, you practice and two, you consume the necessary power nutrients to do that.

If you use the physical world as the example, then the same two steps can apply to the strength of character. The way you achieve and master it is to practice with increasing resistance, and by consuming the proper nutrients. The nutrients, in this case, are books and articles of inspiration by men that have gone before you - men of profound character and accomplishment sow the seeds of motivation that can aid in the building and refining of your strength. If you haven't had men like this in your life, who could lead by example, there is still hope because there are many real men out there. As we become adults we get to choose. As adults, we are now in control of what we will become, and we can find others who inspire us and follow in their footsteps.

As you improve, treat every mistake, downfall, and failure as opportunities to grow stronger, while you learn the nature of things around you and develop your standards as a man. There is no such thing as a waste of time due to failure. There is no failure that is permanent unless we cease to learn from our mistakes.

As a person of character, you are seeking a pathway to strength in every endeavor you make, in every act you commit, and with every word you utter. Examine your strength by looking at it in the silence of your reflection and use it to your benefit. Do not squander these opportunities (mistakes, downfalls, and failures) by allowing your ego to get defensive and convince you to deny mistakes. Convert each mistake, each step in toil, into an equivalent strength. Use it.

***

Chapter 9: Real Men, Defined by You

I asked others: "What is your definition of a real man? Or can you give an example."

Here are the responses I received.

1. A considerate, caring, unconditional lover, and a protector.

2. To me, a real man would be one that wants to make sure I'm okay and protected. Cares about what I think or do. Doesn't denigrate and doesn't criticize me because I'm not perfect. Loves me for who I am. And always has my back. But above all, just wants to be with me and spend time with me. Respect, love, protect and care about me. Because if he were in my life, he would have all of that in return and more.

3. I thought I knew once, but it was all a dream.

4. A real man keeps his word. He is kind, gentle and strong. He never strikes a woman or child. He is a protector of his family. He is slow to anger and thinks before he speaks. He doesn't go out of his way to fight but won't back down either. He respects women and treats them as his equal.

5. This only exists in books. Sadly, real men are now a part of history.

6. Who really knows in the modern world? Men keep getting told they're not allowed to behave like men. Everyone's confused about who they are nowadays because of all this PC stuff.

7. A man is someone who is attentive, honest, loyal. A man is someone who can hold you up, but not hold you back. But, the best for me is the way he loves our sons.

8. God fearing man of his words. Then everything else falls into place. The respect. The success. The love of a real woman.

9. He's considerate, he's understanding and just AWESOME!!

10. A man who does not build himself up at the expense of others. Nor wield power to control and denigrate others. A man who can choose wisdom over force. Who can laugh at himself. A man who falls in love, and knows how to be romantic. A person who is a positive role model to young people.

11. Secure in his masculinity to be kind. Intelligent without bragging condensation. Owns his shortcomings.

12. GI Joe, that's as real as it gets.

13. It's kind of circular reasoning, but a real man is someone a caring parent would point out to their son and say, "Grow up to be like him." Having strength but never using it to hurt anyone. Fictional versions: Atticus Finch, Captain America, Aragorn, Superman until the last few horrible movies.

14. Any type of description would be biased, as morality and what is right or wrong is subjective to many. In my humble opinion, a man is someone who is capable of standing alone in the right, but does not ever turn away from a person who is willing to help or one who is in need. Is able to ride into a storm, but does not do so recklessly or without a contingency plan when things go wrong. A man has the aura of being strong of will and mind, even if not strong of body, has the determination to see anything through with or without aid, and has the character to accept help with gratitude and honor while not acting vulnerable or being incapable. One that steps up to do something without needing instructions.

15. One that steps up to do something without needing instructions.

16. Handle your business as a man does, care for others, know who you are.

17. Doesn't cheat, steal, or lie.

18. Someone with a Y chromosome. *Someone responded to that: ANNNNH! WRONG The question asked: REAL MAN. You have to admit that there are plenty of 'Y'ers that do not fit that description.

19. Is his own best self...whatever he feels that is.

20. I'm old school. I have good manners, I show others respect and I will always help those who need me. It's not because I'm old fashioned, it's because I was raised properly.

21. That is a really good question and all I can say there are many facets to a real man but one of many is to be able to show emotions if a man feels that it is weak to show emotions you need worry a little.

22. Strong to defend those weaker, yet still kind. A seeker of the truth.

23. Maturity. Perceptions. Wisdom.

24. A sharing and caring and nurturing soul that always has weed?

25. Immoveable on major principles, but not sweating the small stuff.

26. Is there one out there?!

27. Clint Eastwood. He is NOT alpha.

28. One who covers and prays for his family.

29. Strong enough to defend what he knows is important. Smart enough to know when to use it.

Chapter 10: You Have What It Takes

"You can't relate to a superhero, to a superman, but you can identify with a real man who in times of crisis draws forth some extraordinary quality from within himself and triumphs." ~ Timothy Dalton

We all have what it takes to level up and become better human beings. That's what evolving is all about. Once we know and learn what qualities the people we look up to possess, then we can follow in similar footsteps. It's about raising our standards, and rising to the occasion. It's as simple and easy as that. Then, with a little follow through, you will be closer to reaching your full potential. You will become a good example for others. Here are a few things that define a real man; a person with integrity. Of course, the list may vary, and it may not be complete, but you get the general idea. It's not complicated. If you haven't been given the best examples in life, but you have stumbled upon this book, then your inner being knows there's so much more available to you, and wants you to have it.

When you rise above mediocrity, life becomes absolutely amazing. Enjoy this awesome journey.

Here are some traits of a real man.

He knows what he wants and goes after it

Boys complain while men take action. He finds a solution instead of complaining. A real man takes initiative and is decisive. He's not wishy-washy. He knows what he wants and isn't afraid to work hard and go after it. He knows it won't be easy, but he sets goals and follows through. He knows nothing in life, worth having, is easy, and he has the self-discipline and wisdom to do what it takes.

He is a true gentleman.

Manners are not a thing of the past for a real man. A real man makes eye contact when speaking with someone and shows respect to everyone. He is not just friendly with the people he admires. He treats every single person he meets with the same amount of respect. He treats others the way he'd like to be treated. He treats others the way he'd like his daughter and/or mother to be treated. He opens the doors for women and children, doesn't use profanity in front of women and children, and follows the 'ladies before gentlemen' sentiment. This means while ordering at a restaurant – a real man lets a woman order first before he blurts out what he wants, and he will not walk out a door before a woman either, instead, he will hold it open and let her go first.

He has self-respect

A real man sees through the façade of advertising companies that promote unhealthy items and peer pressure has no effect on him. He knows who he is and is proud of it. A real man takes care of himself; mind, body, and soul. He knows his limits, has self-discipline, and doesn't poison his body with junk food, cigarettes, alcohol, or drugs. He likes to exercise and eat right because he likes to be on the top of his game always. He strives to keep his mind and body strong and healthy. He knows bad habits hold him back and can turn into addictions. He doesn't waste time yet values it and puts electronics away. He creates good habits and keeps them. He knows what needs to be done, therefore, he does it.

He does what he says and always tells the truth

You can trust a real man. If he says he will be there, he will be there. He does what he says he will do and he never lies. He doesn't fib, tell little white lies, or exaggerate. A real man is strong enough to tell the truth. He thinks before he speaks. You know a real man will always strive to do the right thing. He is authentic. You don't have to doubt or question what a real man says.

He is a giver

He will give you the shirt off his back - or his belt if you need it. (In the testimonies you'll read about a real man who just reached down and took his belt right off his pants for someone.) A real man is not selfish or lazy and puts others first.

He is supportive and won't quit on you

A real man is confident in who he is and doesn't allow insecurities or jealousy to get the best of him. He knows how to handle his emotions. He supports the people he loves and will not quit on them.

He is solution oriented and has a positive mindset

A real man knows that being solution oriented requires focus, and is a great tool for bettering one's life. He finds the positive in all things and uses it to his advantage. He sets goals and always strives to accomplish them. He knows that great things take time.

He is mature

A real man doesn't manipulate others, take revenge, or try to deceive anyone. He can remain calm and peaceful even in the most chaotic and trying times. Although he may be freaking out on the inside, he holds it together and can be counted on. A real man doesn't get defensive and owns up to his mistakes. A boy gets defensive and makes excuses, while a real man admits when he is wrong and does better next time.

He's not afraid to cry and loves easily

A real man isn't afraid to cry or show his emotions. He feels his feelings and learns from them. He may be scared but he feels the fear and does it anyway. True bravery is facing our fear and pushing through it, time and time again. A real man isn't afraid to show that he cares. He will hug the people he cares about and is not ashamed to do so.

He takes responsibility and is quick to apologize

A real man takes full responsibility for his part in all situations. He is quick to say he is sorry if he is wrong, and to make things better. But he never apologizes for who he is. He knows who he is and what he stands for.

He knows how to lighten up, laugh, and play

A real man knows that life is meant to be enjoyed. He makes time to stop and smell the roses. When he is working, he works, and when he is playing, he plays. He is adventurous. He doesn't take life too seriously and knows how to have fun. A real man isn't grumpy, and has a great sense of humor. He is witty and clever. He knows that it's great to aspire to new heights, but that when we take it all too seriously it can end up feeling like a burden.

He reflects and is appreciative

A real man takes time to be still and meditate on good things. He is grateful. He wakes up ready to face the day and retires in the evening on a good note reflecting on all that he is thankful for.

***

Chapter 11: Testimonies

THE FOLLOWING ARE TRUE TESTIMONIES submitted by people who are learning what being a real man entails. Some of these testimonies give examples of what a real man is, and others are examples of what a real man is not. We can learn from both. I wish I could share all the testimonies that were submitted, and I thank all who shared their stories. My team and I picked a few testimonies that we thought others could relate to most.

Not all of us have been blessed with the best role models. This is not about blaming our parents or relatives because we are all human and we all make mistakes, but positive or negative role models definitely make a difference in how our lives turn out. It has been proven time and time again that children mimic and copy what they see. Children learn and follow the habits of their parents. Lackful habits, unhealthy habits, and harmful habits will unintentionally, but automatically be passed on. As adults, we sense that there is more and that there may be better ways of living our lives. We want to thrive; to evolve and become better for generations to come.

Testimony 1

Dear Sage,

Thank you for allowing me to submit a testimony on what I think makes a real man. When I think of what makes a real man, a relative of mine quickly pops into my head. Joe is strong, brave, and always puts others first. He doesn't waste his time fighting or arguing about petty things. He respects other people's differing opinions and moves on. He is a supportive husband and father and provides for his family. Joe was in the Army and maybe he learned a lot about becoming a real man from being put in the situations that the military requires one to be in. Maybe he learned discipline and self-control through that. I'm not exactly sure, but I think he has always been the type of man who wants to do better for himself and for his family. I've never seen Joe mad or angry. He is always calm and level headed. I don't think I've ever heard him use foul language. He is a pilot and people put their lives in his hands on a regular basis. We recently had a major snowstorm and had to travel out of town. Joe was driving so there wasn't an ounce of worry about it. We know that with Joe driving, we will be safe. If anyone else would have been behind the wheel, we would've been nervous wrecks.

I was working with Joe another time while he was helping one of his neighbors cut down a large oak tree. Joe was using his chainsaw and getting the job done. Again, another example of a real man. I was inspired that he even offered. It was his day off and he noticed his neighbor was outside working on the tree. He could have just driven by but instead offered his help and spent four hours working on sawing and clearing that tree up. When we took a coffee break, his neighbor mentioned that he liked Joe's belt and told him he had been looking for one like it for a while. Joe reached down, undid his belt, and gave it to his neighbor, no questions asked. Who does that? A real man does. He is giving and kind, yet strong and powerful.

Just last week, I went with Joe and some other family members to see a live band that was playing in the area. We all jumped in Joe's large SUV and he drove. When we got to the restaurant he held the door for everyone. When we were about to place our order, he made sure all the women ordered first. And when we finally left for the night, I watched as he opened and held the back door of his SUV for the ladies to get in. He didn't just get in the driver's seat and wait. Instead, he opened the car door and closed it for the women we were with.

Joe takes care of his body and works out doing things he enjoys. Hiking and biking often. I think this is another example of a real man. One who takes care of himself. He is responsible and doesn't overindulge in alcohol or junk food. He likes to have fun and have a beer once in a while, but you can be sure that he will always keep himself under control.

He is mature and kind. He thinks before he speaks. I've never seen him be rude or disrespectful to anyone. He has a great sense of humor and likes to laugh.

These are just a few examples of why I think Joe is the definition of a real man. I could go on and on. I didn't grow up with a father around, so watching Joe live such an honorable life doesn't go unnoticed. He inspires me. He makes me want to be a better person. It's almost in everything that he does. He is strong, he is brave, he is generous. His wife and children are so lucky and fortunate to have him. I know his children will follow in his footsteps.

Sincerely,

Tristan R.

Testimony 2

I've been dating a man for over ten years and I'm still hopeful that things will change. I don't think it's his fault entirely that he is the way he is, right? As you've said before, we are who we spend time with. So he couldn't help but be who he is because of the way he was brought up; by his workaholic father who had an affair with a co-worker and left his mother when he was nine years old. So maybe it was his dad who wasn't a real man in the first place, and I don't know about his dad's dad. Who knows where it all began. I want to submit my testimony not out of disrespect but out of hope. I haven't given up on my boyfriend, and I know that all boys have the potential to be men.

When I first started dating my boyfriend, he had recently separated from his high-school sweetheart. She didn't treat him well and he really needed to vent about it. She had fallen in love with someone else and told him that she loved him more like a family member and not a lover. He was devastated and more than ready to move on. We had fun together. The beginning of our relationship was amazing. I fell in love with him quickly and really liked being with him. He has so many great qualities.

When his ex-girlfriend found out that he was dating me, she started contacting him more. She'd need him to go to her place to help fix the water heater or the leaky sink. So funny how that happens, that some people don't appreciate what they have until someone else wants it. So, she started calling him and asking him to come to her rescue. The next thing I knew she was calling my phone number and leaving messages crying. I called her back and we had a good and mature conversation. I heard her out and she told me that she wanted him back. I told her that I respected that but what she was telling me wasn't what I was hearing from my boyfriend, and that he and I were in a really good place. She went on to tell me that the weekend before, when he was there helping her with her lawn mower, that they made out; they kissed a lot on the staircase and that he had an erection but wouldn't have sex with her because he was now dating me. This was news to me and I was completely surprised. I was upset and confronted my boyfriend about it. I told him that I was a big girl and that I could handle the truth. I told him that I can understand how these things happen. They had been together for a long time. I just wanted him to be honest with me and tell me the truth. I told him that we could move pass it if he told me the truth, and I meant it. He denied it flat out and said that his ex girlfriend lies all the time; that I couldn't trust anything she said. He said this over and over. I wanted to believe him but something just didn't sit right with me about it. Something seemed off. In my mind, something just wasn't making sense. If his ex-girlfriend wasn't being honest then why would she say that he stopped himself and wouldn't go any further? She could have made up so much more if it wasn't true. Instead, she told me they kissed a lot, she felt his erection and wanted to go further but that he said he couldn't because he was dating me. It sounded like the truth to me. She also told me that he told her he wished he could date both of us at the same time. Another thing he denied and said was a lie. So those were the first lies that I know about. It took four months for him to finally admit that his ex-girlfriend was telling the truth. I basically hounded him in the nicest ways possible until he came clean. I knew deep down that she was telling the truth and that he wasn't.

In those four months, we became very serious and had moved in together. I forgave him and we moved on from this dishonesty situation. But for some strange reason, the dishonesty issue continued through the years and about the littlest things, too.

One time, after a long drive, he came home and I asked if he had eaten yet and he quickly said no. Later that day, I found a receipt that showed he had picked up fast food right beforehand. Something so little, and I just don't understand the need to lie about such things. I wouldn't have cared less if he had eaten. I called him on it and he just made an excuse. That's another thing, he gives excuse after excuse; silly excuse after silly excuse, when he lies. It can be very frustrating.

He didn't tell me that he had a massive amount of debt until after we had purchased a house together. Things like that.

I forgive time and time again because there are so many good things about him, and we get along so well and now here we are ten years later. I love him very much but the lying all the time seems somewhat boyish and it's hard to believe anything that he says now.

He doesn't always do what he says, doesn't follow through on ideas all the time; he often repeats himself over and over, he often talks only about himself. He doesn't apologize easy and often blames others for things he does. He doesn't take responsibility for his part in things. He doesn't open the door for me, enters buildings first, walks in front of me, acts like a defensive 10-year-old boy when we argue, and can be rude and sarcastic often. He doesn't think before he speaks and says the rudest things at times. He can act like a sad little boy if he doesn't get his way, BUT he makes me laugh and is a great friend and lover. He is smart, caring, helpful, funny, cooks, knows how to work hard, and, I know, means well overall. He has a good heart and I'm not giving up on him.

I guess my testimony is in hope that others will read this and see how damaging lying can be. I am also hopeful that my boyfriend will continue to grow the more and more his dishonesty, sarcasm, and immaturity comes to light. And the more and more I forgive it. That is my hope anyway.

With gratitude,

Jennifer G.

Testimony 3

What makes a real man? I'd like to give an example. A real man is someone like my brother, Shawn. I've looked up to him my whole life. He owns a very successful business that he started on his own when he was just 20 years old. When someone calls him, he never procrastinates and returns their phone call right away. Just last week he received a text from a client in need. He returned their phone call within three minutes and was at their office within ten. He spent the next two hours with this client and helped solve their problem.

He is a dedicated father and was a dedicated husband (before his wife left him for another man) - which is another example of his loyalty. His wife was unfaithful on several occasions throughout their marriage and many people knew it, including Shawn, but he continued to love, cherish, and forgive his wife time and time again. Eventually, she told him that she wanted a divorce and he granted her her wish just as he had always done all throughout their marriage. He took his vows seriously and gave her whatever she wanted. He was loyal right to the end. It took a year for the divorce to finalize but he didn't take off his wedding ring or even consider dating anyone else, until it was official, even though she had clearly moved on with someone else.

He looks you in the eye when he is talking to you and gives you his full attention. He is kind and generous, loyal and trustworthy, strong and courageous. He is the definition of a real man.

Best regards,

Steven T.

Testimony 4

Dear Sage,

I've appreciated being a client of yours over the year. I appreciate your nonjudgment. You've been very helpful. When you sent out the request for "Real Man" testimonies I felt drawn to send in my own.

As you know, I've struggled in my romantic relationships. I keep seeming to make the same mistakes over and over, and often times with married men. I don't know why I fall for them. I don't know why I flirt with them. I don't know why I believe them. I don't know why I feel drawn to them. I don't know why I let it happen over and over. I'm tired of it. These married men are cowards. They are not real men at all.

Through the years, I've flirted with several married men and most of the time they return the flirtatious nature. And as you know, many situations turn serious and little by little we become romantically involved.

But there was this one guy who I tried to pursue who wouldn't have it. I felt drawn to him – he was gorgeous, and he always smelled so good. He was smart and funny and had a smile to die for. Every time he walked into the room, I felt lighter, happier. He was tall, dark, and handsome, and through the years of working with him I'd repeatedly flirt, hint, touch, and email him through interoffice mail in the hopes that he would respond in a way that might lead to more. But I got nothing. At first, he was nice about it and would just ignore me, then he started being short with me and even seemed to avoid me. Eventually, he told me flat out to stop.it. He said that he was a married man, and although that might not mean anything to me, it certainly meant something to him. He took his vows seriously and he said that each day he woke up and thought about the promise that he made to his wife. He reminded himself every morning of the commitment he made and why. He thought it was important to share everything with his wife, including all of the advances I had been making. I was shocked. No one had ever really put me in my place like that before. I believe this is the definition of a real man. One who doesn't let his ego get the best of him. One who honors his word. One who doesn't back down from doing the right thing.

This encounter really made me question everything. It made me see that the men who respond positively to my advances are really boys. They are immature jerks who don't have a backbone. They are weak. They are cowards. They are the reason I don't dare to get involved in a committed relationship. I've seen too much. I've seen through the years that real men are rare.

But more importantly, I've learned from this. I've learned what to look for. I will be able to see with open eyes now when I come across a real man. And I will also be able to see the cowards and choose to walk in the other direction. Thank you for allowing me to share my story. I am ready for a real man.

Best,

Kristina W.

Testimony 5

It wasn't until I started working and volunteering at my church that I discovered what a real man is. There was one guy I worked with and he showed me, through our everyday interactions, what a real man is. He never walked in a door before a woman. I even tried to trick him at different times – I would hold the door as wide open as it would go and stand back at the edge of the door, indicating that he could go first, but he would just pause and put his hand way above my head and hold the door and tell me to go first.

We were in a meeting once and there weren't enough chairs for everyone and he offered up his seat in an instant.

We were at a restaurant once and it was cold, and he offered me his jacket.

We watched a movie as a group one evening, and there was a scene where the actress was wearing a bikini, and I noticed that this guy looked away from the screen. I discovered that there is a huge difference between men with integrity and men without. What a difference!

He is kind to everyone he meets and amazingly kind to his family as well. I've never seen him get angry or lose his temper in any way.

A real man is one who has Christian values. The Bible lays it out very simply and if one follows these insights then one will live a successful and satisfying life.

Sin leads to destruction and obedience, in doing what is right, leads to blessing after blessing. It's very easy to understand.

Here are just a few quotes that discuss what a real man is.

"When I was a child, I spoke as a child, I felt as a child, I thought as a child. Now that I have become a man, I have put away childish things." ~ 1 Corinthians 13:11

"Watch ye, stand fast in the faith, do manfully, and be strengthened." ~ 1 Corinthians 16:13

"In all things showing yourself an example of good works; in your teaching showing integrity, seriousness, incorruptibility," ~ Titus 2:7

Yours respectfully,

Mia R.

Conclusion

A man is not the sum of his genetic code. A man is not the collection of his physical attributes. A man is not the outline of his professional achievements, and not the treasury of his financial gains. So, then, what is a man?

A man is one half of the equation that gives rise to the foundation of his family. He is the half that brings responsibility, trustworthiness, loyalty, and strength to the union. The man, together with his partner, provides the foundation to raise a family that will extend into the next generation and fulfill the purpose of every soul on earth.

Being a man is not as hard as one may think, neither is it as easy as one might expect if they have the wrong sense of objectives. Being a man is about contributing selflessly and finding his purpose in that contribution.

When we look at the universe we see that we are all connected. Humans are connected to each other by bonds that are both physical and emotional. We are connected to the earth and the earth is connected to space and we make up the universe. Just as a tree is a part of this universe, but serves a function, man too is connected to the universe and serves a function. This function is what we term as purpose and each man is endowed with the skills that make this purpose come to life.

But to do that - to make the purpose alive, we need to understand ourselves. That is what this book has attempted to do. We have laid out the facts in the way that we hope will get you to think, reflect, and meditate on the truth of the universe and your purpose is a way that is customized to who you are. We are the direct results of our upbringing, but we don't always have good role models in life. When you become an adult, you can shape your life as you desire. It's not about blame, it's about doing better than those who came before us. It's not about *trying* to do better, it's about *doing* better. We better ourselves and in the process create a most wonderful life, and one in which we can be proud of.

***

About Sage Wilcox

Sage Wilcox is an author and certified energy healer and teacher. Sage enjoys traveling and giving advice to clients, friends, and family on healing, love, and relationships. Sage also enjoys studying human behavior, reading, writing, being outdoors, and enhancing relationships with others. Sage enjoys growing closer to the Divine Source and has discovered, the more we learn and practice The Word, the better life becomes. Sage is a hopeless romantic and strives to help others fall madly in love with everything about their lives! There's no room for boring in Sage's life. Sage likes to spice life up in every way! In Sage's words: "We can learn so much from each other. Here's to growing and learning, one step at a time. Let's manifest well-being, love, and unity! Let's get passionate!"

Please consider leaving a book review and visit:
http://sagewilcox.wix.com/books
www.facebook.com/sagewilcoxbooks
www.findyourwaypublishing.com

Thank you!

Would you please consider leaving reviews, online, for my books? Reviews help more than you know, and don't have to be long; a few sentences will do. Thank you very much for your time and consideration. I am sincerely grateful.

Wishing many blessings to you and yours,

~Sage

Other books by Sage Wilcox:

Nonfiction:

Love Letters from Exes: *Proof That Life Goes on After a Break Up and Love Is What You Make It*

Get It Up: *101 Ways to Raise Your Vibration, Reduce Stress, Depression, & Anxiety, Increase Joy, Peace, & Happiness and Attract Abundance Automatically!*

The 2-Hour Vacation: *Let Go and Relax, Reduce Stress & Anxiety, Gain Inner Peace, and Happiness*

The Importance of Doing It: *How to Utilize Discipline to Get Out of Bed, and Make Your Dreams Come True! A Guide to Taking Action to Create Successful Habits…*

Less Is Best: *Declutter, Organize, & Simplify to Reach Minimalism; Get More Time, Money, & Energy*

You Had Me at Re: Hello: *The Ultimate Guide to Online Dating, Including Tips and Testimonies*

Neuroplasticity and the Default Mind: *How to Shape Your Plastic Brain by Forming New Connections to Automatically Get Positive Results, Success and Prosperity*

Adjust: *How to Conquer and Accept Change and Adversity Swiftly; Stop Putting off the Love, Money, Peace, Success, and Happiness You Deserve Now*

Born New: *How to See the Familiar with New Eyes, Embrace the Magic of the Present Moment, Experience Satisfaction and Joy like Never Before*

Romance Books by S. J. Wilcox :

Until We Fall

Under the Covers

Solitary Heart

Awakened Heart

Disclaimer

The purpose of this book is for entertainment purposes only. This book is designed to provide information and motivation to our readers. The content is the sole expression and opinion of its author, and not necessarily that of the publisher. The testimonies contained in this book are from contributors and are the contributor's recollections of their experiences. This is a work based on opinions, recollections, and true events, however, names, characters, businesses, places, and incidents are either the products of the authors' imaginations or used in a fictitious manner. Any resemblance to actual persons, living or dead, businesses, companies, events, locales, or actual events is entirely coincidental. This book is not intended nor is it implied to be a substitute for professional medical advice, and any medical advice and any medical information contained in this book is not intended to be diagnostic or treatment in any way. The author and publisher are not engaged in rendering medical, psychological, legal, or any other professional services. If medical, psychological or other expert assistance is required, please talk to your physician and locate the services of a competent professional. The author and publisher shall have neither liability nor responsibility to any person or entity with respect to any loss or damage caused, or alleged to have been caused, directly or indirectly, by the information contained in this book. Neither the publisher nor the individual author(s) shall be liable for any physical, psychological, emotional, financial, or commercial damages, including, but not limited to, special, incidental, consequential or other damages. Our views and rights are the same: You are responsible for your own choices, actions, and results. If you do not wish to be bound by the above, you may return this book along with a copy of the receipt to the publisher for a full refund.